JUV/E
N
6999
.C46
M35
2004

SSHORE

Chicago Public Library

R0406209745
Dreamer from the village : the story of

P9-DEF-863

SOUTH SHORE BRANCH
2505 EAST 73rd STREET
CHICAGO, ILLINOIS 60649

To my parents, Bea and Bud Markel
—M. M.

To Lucy Clara Merriam Jones
—E. L.

ILLUSTRATOR'S NOTE

The images that I have painted are not intended to be historically or biographically accurate. They were based not on photographs or written accounts, but on Chagall's own paintings, which reflected his feeling and his particular way of seeing. Thus Chagall painted green cows, Bella floating in the sky, himself with neon-blue hair. Without actually copying his work, I tried to capture some of that feeling and to communicate, as the text says, that Marc saw things others didn't see.

Permission is gratefully acknowledged for the use of *I and the Village* (p. 36):
© 2004 Artists Rights Society (ARS), New York / ADAGP, Paris

Henry Holt and Company, LLC, *Publishers since 1866*
115 West 18th Street, New York, New York 10011
www.henryholt.com

Henry Holt is a registered trademark of Henry Holt and Company, LLC

Text copyright © 2005 by Michelle Markel. Illustrations copyright © 2005 by Emily Lisker
All rights reserved. Distributed in Canada by H. B. Fenn and Company Ltd.

Library of Congress Cataloging-in-Publication Data
Markel, Michelle. Dreamer from the village: the story of Marc Chagall /
by Michelle Markel; illustrated by Emily Lisker.—1st ed.
p.   cm.
Summary: Chronicles the life of Marc Chagall, a celebrated
twentieth-century artist who was born in Russia.
ISBN-13: 978-0-8050-6373-8
ISBN-10: 0-8050-6373-0
1. Chagall, Marc, 1887– —Juvenile literature.
2. Artists—Russia (Federation)—Biography—Juvenile literature.
[1. Chagall, Marc, 1887– 2. Artists.] I. Lisker, Emily, ill. II. Title.
N6999.C46M35 2004   709'.2—dc22   2003022498

First Edition—2005 / Designed by Donna Mark
The artist used acrylic on canvas to create the illustrations for this book.
Printed in the United States of America on acid-free paper. ∞
10 9 8 7 6 5 4 3 2 1

DREAMER FROM THE VILLAGE
THE STORY OF MARC CHAGALL

SOUTH SHORE BRANCH
2505 EAST 73rd STREET
CHICAGO, ILLINOIS 60649

MICHELLE MARKEL · ILLUSTRATED BY EMILY LISKER

HENRY HOLT AND COMPANY · NEW YORK

R0406209745

Long ago, on the plains of Russia, there was a village of dirt roads and timber houses. One day, while a fire raged through the town, a sickly baby was born. His mother kept him safe in a feeding trough.

The baby was named Moshe, but later he was called Marc. As a little boy he roamed the streets, clutching a hunk of buttered bread in his fist. Rabbis and schoolboys walked off to *heder*, musicians and tradesmen trotted past, and women came out of shops, their baskets laden with cones of sugar and candles wrapped in blue paper.

Marc climbed up to his attic window to get a better view. The town was like a richness that filled him—the goats and chickens, the factories, the cemetery, and everything that lay beyond.

Sometimes Marc even crawled up on the roof. After all, his grandpa used to do it. Marc heard that on Sukkoth or Simchas Torah, the old man could be found perched on the chimney pipe, munching carrots, especially in nice autumn weather.

The seasons brought wondrous holidays. On Passover, Marc loved the colorful pictures in the Haggadah. He loved the deep violet of the wine in his father's glass. And when he opened the door for the prophet Elijah, silver stars trembled on a velvet spring sky.

Marc knew he was different from other boys. He saw things they didn't see. On the Sabbath, enchanted by the singing of prayers, Marc saw houses floating.

Once, as his uncle fiddled him a tune, the ceiling opened. Marc saw the clouds in the evening sky and smelled the stable and the fields.

And one afternoon, the color of his uncle's skin drifted out the window, onto the street, and rested on the cupola of the church.

Marc decided he was meant for something special. He didn't want a life like his father's. His papa rose at dawn to pray in temple, then spent the day hauling barrels of herring at a factory. At night he came home with frozen hands, clothes wet with brine, too tired to eat his dinner.

At *heder* Marc forgot his lessons an hour after he learned them. In high school he failed all his subjects but drawing and geometry, the study of shapes. What was to become of the boy?

The circles, lines, and angles seemed to take
him somewhere. Using burlap bags for canvas,
Marc began to draw.

He hung his pictures on the wall for everyone to see. But his family didn't like them. An uncle was afraid to shake his hand because making images was a sin. Once, after the floor was washed, Marc's sisters took his sketches off the wall, laid them down, and wiped their shoes on them.

But Marc kept drawing. One day, as his mother was making bread, he seized her floury elbow and cried, "I want to be a painter. I can't be a clerk in a warehouse, or an accountant, or a butcher. Save me!"

His mother sent him to art school. The teacher told him to draw neat copies of plaster statues. The paint was the color of tobacco stains. But Marc wanted to draw villagers and peasants, with loose, clumsy lines—and a touch of violet.

Marc took more art lessons in St. Petersburg. He didn't
have the money for a room, so he shared beds with people,
slept on their couches or in cubbyholes under their stairs.
He could only dream of bread and sausages.

But when Marc painted he was happy. Something always
wanted to be painted. His village. The factories, his
grandpa's house, even funerals that he'd watched. In one
scene, the sad sky turned greenish yellow, and a lonely
fiddler crouched on a roof.

During a visit home Marc met a woman named Bella. She was rich and wanted to be an actress. The two of them walked on a bridge, watching the clouds change shapes. They fell in love.

Deep inside, Marc knew he was talented, but from teachers he could learn nothing more. He'd seen pictures from Paris, the art center of the world. Marc packed his paint box, his tubes of paint—everything he owned—and took the train to France.

Paris was a thrill. In Russia the sky was weak and dreary, but here the sun bathed everything in light. Marc rushed through the Louvre, to see all the paintings. He spent hours in art galleries, staring at the pictures. Some had bold colors and tilting shapes. They gave him ideas.

Marc rushed to his studio. He painted till the sun came up, on sheets, tablecloths, even nightshirts.

Goats and milkmaids flew above his village. A jewel-green man talked to a see-through cow. A poet's head spun around as he wrote his poem, and the air shattered into windowpanes of color. This was not the way things really looked—it was how they made him feel.

Years went by. Finally a gallery invited Marc
to have a one-man show. But Marc didn't want to
stay in Paris. He missed Bella. Leaving his pictures
at the gallery, he headed home to Russia.

On his birthday Bella came over. When he opened the door for her, he saw blue air, love, and flowers float in. Three weeks later they had a wedding. Happy couples soared through Marc's canvases. The village shone like an emerald.

A great war broke out, keeping Marc and his bride in Russia. At first he painted everything that passed by his window—the rabbis and the beggars and the sad old men. Some glowed red, others green. But soon he couldn't paint, because he had to work to feed his family.

One day, eight years after he'd left France, Marc
received a letter from an old friend. "Are you still
alive?" it said. "Do you know that you're famous
here? Your pictures are selling for high prices."

People smiled at Marc's magic animals. They sighed at the miracles of his village. His blooming colors filled their hearts with moods. No one had ever painted like this before.

Marc moved back to France. He was finally able to earn a living doing what he'd always loved.

He worked until he was an old man.

When he was ninety Marc received a wonderful
invitation. The Louvre wanted him to show his paintings.
On opening day Marc went to the museum. He had gone
there long ago because his teachers didn't understand
what he was doing. He'd been trying to paint the feelings
he carried in his heart ever since he was a little boy. For
Marc that was always the most important thing. It made
him one of the greatest painters in the world.

Author's Note

Several incidents in this story, especially the ones that take place during Marc Chagall's childhood, are based on those described in his autobiography, *My Life*.

More About Marc Chagall

Marc Chagall was one of the first artists to express the inner world of dreams, fantasies, and memories. His work is known for its luminous colors and magical imagery.

The artist was born on July 7, 1887, near Vitebsk, in the western province of the Russian empire now known as Belarus. His given name was Moshe Segal, later changed to the French Marc Chagall. He grew up in a devoutly religious Jewish atmosphere, which later became the subject matter for much of his work.

When he was nineteen Chagall went to St. Petersburg to take art lessons. With the aid of a generous patron, he moved to Paris, the art center of the Western World. Chagall was influenced by the vivid colors and geometric structures of Cubism and other modern techniques but went on to develop his own kind of painting.

A Berlin art gallery organized Chagall's first one-man show in 1914. In the same year, he made a trip to Russia, unaware that the outbreak of World War I would prevent his

Marc Chagall, *I and the Village*. 1911. Oil on canvas, 6' 3 5/8" x 59 5/8". Mrs. Simon Guggenheim Fund. (146.1945) The Museum of Modern Art, New York, NY. Digital image © The Museum of Modern Art/Licensed by SCALA/Art Resource, NY.

return. His marriage to Bella Rosenfeld inspired a series of fantasy paintings about their love. After the Russian Revolution in 1917, Chagall became the commissar of fine arts and later, director of a local art academy.

In the years after his return to Paris in 1923, Chagall became a well-regarded lithographer. During World War II he lived in the United States, designing sets and costumes for the ballet.

Chagall moved back to France after the war ended. Among the works he created in his later years were the ceiling painting of the Paris Opera, murals for the Metropolitan Opera in New York City, stained glass windows for the Hadassah Hebrew University in Jerusalem, and mosaics and tapestries for the Israeli parliament building.

At the age of ninety Chagall became one of very few living artists to be exhibited at the Louvre, the famous art museum he had visited as a young man on his first trip to Paris. He worked almost until his death on March 28, 1985.

He had this advice about painting: "You must work the painting with the thought that something of your soul penetrates it and gives it substance. A picture should be born and bloom like a living thing. It should seize some soft and unseizable something, the allure and profound meaning of whatever interests you."

GLOSSARY

Haggadah (hah-GAH-duh) • A prayer book used during the ritual seder meal of Passover, a seven-day holiday that celebrates the Jews' freedom from slavery in ancient Egypt.

Heder (HAY-dur) • Jewish elementary school. Also known as *cheder*.

Simchas Torah (SIM-cuss TOR-uh) • This holiday celebrates the Torah, the first five books of the Old Testament. Also known as Simchat Torah in modern Hebrew.

Sukkoth (sook-OTE) • An eight-day fall harvest festival. Also called Sukkot or Sukkos.